Contents

Some words are shown in bold, **like this**.
You can find them in the glossary on page 23.

What is a roadrunner?

greater roadrunner

A roadrunner is a type of bird.

A bird's body is covered in feathers and most birds can fly.

A Day in the Life: Desert Animals

inner

eri

www.raintreepublishers.co.uk
Visit our website to find out more information about Raintree books.

To order:
☎ Phone 0845 6044371
🖷 Fax +44 (0) 1865 312263
✉ Email myorders@raintreepublishers.co.uk

Customers from outside the UK please telephone +44 1865 312262

Raintree is an imprint of Capstone Global Library Limited, a company incorporated in England and Wales having its registered office at 7 Pilgrim Street, London, EC4V 6LB – Registered company number: 6695582

Text © Capstone Global Library Limited 2011
First published in hardback in 2011
First published in paperback in 2012
The moral rights of the proprietor have been asserted.

Edited by Daniel Nunn, Rebecca Rissman, and Sian Smith
Designed by Richard Parker
Picture research by Elizabeth Alexander
Production by Victoria Fitzgerald
Originated by Capstone Global Library Ltd
Printed and bound in China by South China Printing Company Ltd

ISBN 978 1 406 21965 4 (hardback)
14 13 12 11 10
10 9 8 7 6 5 4 3 2 1

ISBN 978 1 406 22128 2 (paperback)
15 14 13 12
10 9 8 7 6 5 4 3 2 1

British Library Cataloguing in Publication Data

Ganeri, Anita, 1961-
  Roadrunner. -- (A day in the life. Desert animals)
  1. Roadrunner--Juvenile literature.
  I. Title II. Series
  598.7'4-dc22

Acknowledgements

We would like to thank the following for permission to reproduce photographs: Alamy pp. 9, 23 glossary crest (© Rick & Nora Bowers), 10, 21, 23 glossary desert (© John Cancalosi), 11 (© William Leaman), 18 (© Rolf Nussbaumer Photography); FLPA p. 17 (© Bob Langrish); Getty Images pp. 20, 23 glossary cactus (Michael Orton/Photographer's Choice); iStockphoto pp. 13, 23 glossary prey (© Tilmann von Au); Photolibrary pp. 4 (Werner Bollmann/age fotostock), 5 (Thorsten Milse/Picture Press), 8 (David Tipling/OSF), 12 (C. Allan Morgan/Peter Arnold Images), 14, 22 (John Cancalosi/Peter Arnold Images), 15, 19, 23 glossary predator (Wyman Meinzer/Peter Arnold Images), 16 (Michael Sewell/Peter Arnold Images); Shutterstock pp. 7 (© Norman Bateman), 23 glossary insect (© Anke van Wyk), 23 glossary scorpion (© NatalieJean).

Front cover photograph of greater roadrunner (Geococcyx californianus) running in Arizona, USA reproduced with permission of Photolibrary (John Cancalosi/Peter Arnold Images).

Back cover photograph of (left) greater roadrunner looking over its shoulder reproduced with permission of Shutterstock (© Norman Bateman); and (right) roadrunner killing a copperhead snake reproduced with permission of Photolibrary (Wyman Meinzer/Peter Arnold Images).

We would like to thank Michael Bright for his assistance in the preparation of this book.

Every effort has been made to contact copyright holders of material reproduced in this book. Any omissions will be rectified in subsequent printings if notice is given to the publisher.

lesser roadrunner

There are two types of roadrunners.

These are the greater roadrunner and the lesser roadrunner.

Where do roadrunners live?

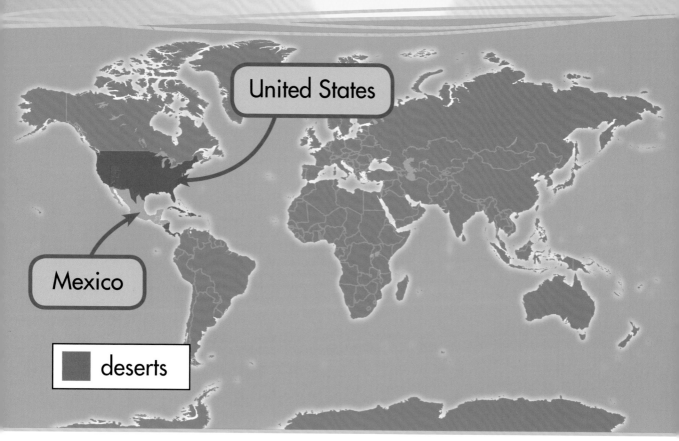

United States

Mexico

deserts

Roadrunners live in the dry **deserts** of the south-west United States and Mexico.

Can you find these deserts on the map?

The desert is very hot in the daytime, but it gets cold at night.

Roadrunners live among the patches of bushes and grass.

What do roadrunners look like?

A roadrunner is about as tall as a chicken.

It has long legs and a long tail.

crest

A roadrunner's feathers are dark brown, with white streaks.

It has a black **crest** of feathers on its head.

What do roadrunners do in the day?

In the morning, roadrunners wake up.

Then they sit in the sun to get warm after the cold **desert** night.

A roadrunner spends most of the day looking for food.

If the weather gets too hot, it rests for a while in the shade.

What do roadrunners eat?

grasshopper

Roadrunners eat lots of different types of food.

They eat **desert insects**, such as grasshoppers, crickets, and beetles.

lizard

Roadrunners sometimes catch lizards, **scorpions**, and snakes.

They also eat mice, spiders, small birds, and prickly pear **cactus**.

How do roadrunners catch food?

In the day, a roadrunner hunts for food on the ground.

It dashes out from behind a bush and catches its **prey**.

snake

If the roadrunner catches a lizard or snake, it bashes it on the ground to kill it.

Then it swallows the animal whole.

How do roadrunners move?

Roadrunners can run fast after their **prey** or away from **predators**.

But they cannot fly very far or well.

As a roadrunner runs, it trails its long tail behind it.

It uses its tail for steering, braking, and balancing.

Where are baby roadrunners born?

nest

A female roadrunner lays her eggs in a nest in a bush or **cactus**.

The nest is above the ground to keep it safe from **predators**.

The male and female take turns to sit on the eggs until they hatch.

For the first few weeks, they bring food for the chicks.

What do roadrunners do at night?

At night, it gets very cold in the **desert**.

Roadrunners shelter among the trees or **cactuses**.

The roadrunners do not sleep but slow their bodies right down.

Next morning, they have to warm up again.

Roadrunner body map

eye

crest

head

wing

feathers

beak

foot

leg

tail

Glossary

 **cactus** prickly plant that grows in the desert

 **crest** group of feathers on a roadrunner's head

 **desert** very dry place that is rocky, stony, or sandy

 **insect** animal that has six legs, such as a grasshopper or beetle

 **predator** animal that hunts other animals for food

 **prey** animal that is eaten by other animals

 **scorpion** animal with eight legs and a curled, stinging tail

Find out more

Books

Desert Animals (Focus on Habitats), Stephen Savage (Wayland, 2006)

Deserts (My World of Geography), Angela Royston (Heinemann Library, 2004)

24 Hours: Desert (Focus on Habitats), Elizabeth Haldane (Dorling Kindersley, 2006)

Websites

Look at some great photos of roadrunners at:
www.avianweb.com/greaterroadrunners.html

Find out all about roadrunners at: www.brookfieldzoo.org/czs/Brookfield/Exhibit-and-Animal-Guide/Feathers-and-Scales/Roadrunner.aspx

Index